# Contents

KT-225-993

# Communism: theory and practice

Communism, in theory, is a system in which there is no private ownership – everyone shares everything. People do the job to which they are best suited for the same reward as everyone else. There is no need for money, and the common good comes before individual wishes.

The most ambitious attempts to establish communism occurred in the 20th century. They were based on the teaching of the German **philosopher** Karl Marx (1818-83), who said that history moved through three stages, from **feudalism**, to **capitalism**, and finally to communism. According to Marx, the **free enterprise**, industrial world of capitalism would inevitably be replaced by communism. The changeover would be marked by a revolution and a **dictatorship** by the **proletariat** (workers) which would allow the establishment of a classless society.

The Russian revolutionary Vladimir Lenin (1870-1924), a follower of Marx's communism ('**Marxism**'), adapted it by saying that a society could progress directly from feudalism to communism, by-passing the capitalist stage. This suited his plans, for capitalism was only just taking root in his native Russia.

## The Soviet Union

In 1917 Lenin masterminded a communist revolution in the Russian Empire, which had been severely crippled by World War I (1914-18). By 1922, after much bitter fighting, the Russian Empire had been replaced by the communist Soviet Union or USSR (Union of Soviet

Supporters of the communist Bolshevik Party march through the streets of Petrograd (St. Petersburg) during the revolution of October 1917 that brought them to power.

Witness to History

# The Collapse of Communism

Stewart Ross

Heinemann
LIBRARY

# www.heinemann.co.uk/library

Visit our website to find out more information about **Heinemann Library** books.

To order:

 Phone 44 (0) 1865 888066

 Send a fax to 44 (0) 1865 314091

💻 Visit the Heinemann Bookshop at www.heinemann.co.uk/library to browse our catalogue and order online.

First published in Great Britain by Heinemann Library,
Halley Court, Jordan Hill, Oxford
OX2 8EJ, part of Harcourt Education.

Heinemann is a registered trademark of
Harcourt Education Ltd.

© Harcourt Education Ltd 2004
First published in paperback in 2005
The moral right of the proprietor has been asserted.

Produced for Heinemann by Discovery Books Ltd
Editorial: Nancy Dickmann, Christine Lawrie and Tanvi Rai
Design: Ian Winton
Picture Research: Rachel Tisdale
Production: Séverine Ribierre

Originated by Dot Gradations Ltd,UK
Printed and bound in China
by South China Printing Company

ISBN 0 431 17065 7 (hardback)
08 07 06 05 04
10 9 8 7 6 5 4 3 2 1

ISBN 0 431 17070 3 (paperback)
09 08 07 06 05
10 9 8 7 6 5 4 3 2 1

**British Library Cataloguing in Publication Data**
Ross, Stewart, 1947–
   The Collapse of Communism. – (Witness to History)
   909.8'29

A full catalogue record for this book is available from the
British Library.

**Acknowledgements**
The publishers would like to thank the following for
permission to reproduce photographs:
Baldwin H. Ward & Kathryn C. Ward/Corbis p.**8**;
Bettmann/Corbis pp.**5**, **28**; Corbis p.**10**; David
Turnley/Corbis pp.**7**, **38**, **51**; Duomo/Corbis p.**25**;
Frederique Gosset/Corbis p.**32**; Hulton-Deutsch
Collection/Corbis p.**18**; Liu Liquin/Corbis p.**49**; Peter
Turnley/Corbis pp.**24**, **26**, **30**, **37**, **43**; Robert Patrick/Corbis
p.**47**; Yevgeny Khaldei/Corbis p.**9**; Popperphoto pp.**4**, **12**, **13**,
**15**, **16**, **17**, **20**, **22**, **27**, **33**, **34**, **36**, **39**, **40**, **41**, **42**, **44**, **48**, **50**.

Cover photograph shows East and West Berliners greeting
each other as the Berlin Wall comes down, November 1989,
reproduced with permission of Robert Maass/Corbis.

The publishers would like to thank Bob Rees, historian and
Assistant Head Teacher, for his assistance in the
preparation of this book.

Every effort has been made to contact copyright holders of
any material reproduced in this book. Any omissions will
be rectified in subsequent printings if notice is given to the
publishers.

The paper used to print this book comes from
sustainable resources.

Words appearing in the text in bold, **like this**, are explained in the glossary.

All Internet addresses (URLs) given in this book were valid at the time of going to press. However, due to
the dynamic nature of the Internet, some addresses may have changed, or sites may have changed or
ceased to exist since publication. While the author and publisher regret any inconvenience this may cause
readers, no responsibility for any such changes can be accepted by either the author or the publisher.

**Socialist Republics**). This was a supposedly voluntary union of communist republics, such as Russia, the Ukraine and Lithuania. However, having gained power through violence, the communists used violence to keep it. Many rights, such as the freedom of speech and the right to travel, were ignored. Those who disagreed with the communist way were imprisoned and often killed.

After the death of Lenin, leadership of the USSR gradually passed to one of his followers, Joseph Dzhugashvili (1928-53), who called himself simply 'Stalin' ('Man of Steel'). Although it was a basic belief of communists that their system would spread world-wide, Stalin accepted that this was unlikely to happen straight away. He concentrated instead on building up the USSR and his own power. All businesses were state-owned and had to follow the government's plans and targets. Agriculture was organized into '**collective farms**' managed by Communist Party officials. Millions of better off peasants opposed Stalin's plans, but he had them killed. He also held the Communist Party in an iron grip. Intellectuals, army officers and others who might oppose him were imprisoned in *gulags* (work camps) or **purged** (forcibly removed or killed). Christianity and other religions were scorned as 'unscientific' and because they encouraged people to accept the injustices of capitalism in favour of rewards in heaven. Communism, in contrast, was held out as rational and practical.

Joseph Stalin (1879-1953), the Soviet dictator from Georgia in the southern USSR. His long and extremely harsh rule, 1928-53, ensured that Soviet communism would forever be associated with tyranny.

The USSR was neutral (did not take sides) at the outbreak of World War II (1939), but in 1941 it was suddenly attacked by Nazi Germany. The Soviets eventually drove out the invader and by May 1945 had advanced far into Eastern Europe. Stalin's communist USSR – **undemocratic** and **tyrannical** – was now a world power and many predicted that Soviet-style communism would indeed take over the world. Communist regimes did take over many countries in Eastern Europe, much of Asia, and countries in South and Central America and Africa. But before the 20th century was out the USSR had collapsed spectacularly and communism seemed a spent cause.

# How do we know?

There are two types of sources that inform us about history: primary and secondary. In the context of the collapse of communism, primary sources come from the time of the collapse. They include anything from personal recollections to government documents. Secondary sources are books, articles, videos, websites and so forth produced by people who have studied the collapse but were not present at the events they are describing. They get their information from both primary sources and other secondary sources.

As with all very recent history, the number and range of sources on the collapse of communism is almost limitless. More than 200 million people were directly affected by the collapse of communist governments in the USSR and neighbouring states in 1989-91. The great majority of them are still alive, each with their own memories and thoughts. A few speak in the pages of this book.

During the collapse, lots of articles were written, speeches made, interviews given. Each of these is a valid primary source, too. So are the many films, TV programmes and photographs from the time. If we add the mass of relevant documents and other material available from the previous 50 years, the sheer quantity of sources becomes even more overwhelming.

People studying translations need to take care because these rarely capture the precise meaning of the original. For example, the Russian word *glasnost*, describing a policy followed by Mikhail Gorbachev (see page 28), is literally translated as 'speaking aloud'. To the Russians it carried a concept of openness not caught in a single English word.

As we all tend to remember only what we want to remember, individual recollections of the fall of communism are often unreliable. There are gaps and inaccuracies. Moreover, many of our sources are based on personal memories of people involved in highly emotional situations, such as imprisonment or liberation from an invader. As a result, these sources will usually carry a personal bias. Finally, personal memories are just that – the thoughts and feelings of one individual. They may or may not be representative of the general mood at the time.

## The clouded truth

The collapse of communism is slowly shifting from current affairs to history. We are still too close to assess sources **objectively**. Only in time will we be able to assess rationally the role of a key figure such as Lech Walesa, for instance (see page 26). Many now see the collapse of communism as a triumph, something that has benefited the human race. Only time will tell whether this is true or not.

A camera crew records the collapse of communism in Germany, 1989. Although TV pictures account for a lot of the primary sources, the vivid images caught on film can mislead historians as much as they inform.

# Communism victorious

In World War II, the **democratic-capitalist** USA and Great Britain were **allied** with the communist **dictatorship** of the USSR. Although representing totally different types of government, they shelved their differences to achieve victory. In February 1945, for instance, President Franklin Roosevelt (USA), Prime Minister Winston Churchill (UK) and Marshal Joseph Stalin (USSR) met to make plans for the post-war world. It was a surprisingly friendly occasion.

By August 1945, however, the mood had changed. Stalin's victorious **Red Army** occupied Eastern Europe and half of Germany. The USA and Britain, whose forces had advanced from the west, feared that Stalin wanted a communist empire in the east. For his part, Stalin was afraid that his former allies might now turn against him.

Beijing, China, June 1949: Communists take over the most populous country on Earth. The picture of Mao Zedong on the front of the **propaganda** truck shows how Chinese communism, like Soviet communism, was based on the **cult** of the supposedly great leader.

Meanwhile, events were taking place elsewhere that would have a huge impact on this **East-West** balance. After the surrender of Germany's ally, Japan, civil war broke out in China between the US-backed Chiang Kai-shek and communist revolutionaries led by Mao Zedong. Mao's forces triumphed, and China became a communist state. So by October 1949, a vast swathe of the Earth's surface, from Beijing, China, to the Baltic Sea, near Sweden, was under communist rule.

This staged propaganda photograph from 2 May 1945 shows a Soviet soldier raising the communist flag over Berlin at the end of World War II in Europe.

## A soldier's view

Writing in the London *Daily Sketch* on 8 May 1945, Brigadier J.G. Smyth considers how East and West will get along in time of peace.

### A Cloud on the Victory Horizon –

The good relations which have been established during the war between ourselves and the United States will endure … because of the feelings of friendship and camaraderie (the goodwill of comrades) established between our fighting men on the field of battle…

But the Russians and ourselves have fought on widely separated battlefields. Our fighting men have never really met and know very little about one another. We must make every effort to get to know the Russians better, not only on the high level of world conferences but on the closer and broader level of a common meeting ground.

### More Visits Needed –

We want exchanges of visits on a large scale, military visits, Press visits, and many more tours by Members of Parliament. Marshal Stalin gave every facility to MPs who visited Russia recently to go where they would and see what they wanted, while Mrs Churchill's gallant and extensive air tour of Russia is an invaluable step in the right direction.

There are suspicions to be broken down on both sides: there are grave language difficulties and many other obstacles to complete understanding. But if the peace we have suffered so much to win is to endure, we must leave no avenue unexplored and consider no endeavour too great.

# An Iron Curtain

In 1950 the collapse of communist rule within 40 years was almost unimaginable. The very opposite appeared more likely: communism seemed the way of the future, advancing inevitably across the world.

By 1946 Europe was dividing into **East** (communist) and **West** (**democratic capitalist**). In 1946, without Soviet help, communists came to power in Yugoslavia and Albania. Soon, other Eastern European countries that were occupied by the **Red Army** during the war also acquired communist governments: Bulgaria (1946), Poland (1947), Romania and Czechoslovakia (1948), and Hungary (1949).

The frontier between East and West was increasingly marked by barbed wire fences and gun towers. These were mainly erected by the East to prevent its citizens fleeing to the West. Noting this, Winston Churchill said that an 'iron curtain' had fallen across the continent. The USA was keen to stop this curtain moving further west.

Despite frequently being introduced by force, communism was often supported by the poorer classes. Such people had nothing to lose – the current system had given them very little, so they were willing to try communism. In 1947, to eliminate the poverty on which communism thrived, the USA began pumping aid worth $13 billion into Western Europe. The USSR was not wealthy enough to do anything similar for the communist **bloc**.

Through the 'iron curtain': this Hungarian family, arriving in Austria in 1956, was one of the many thousands who fled to the West from the communist-governed East during the **Cold War**.

## An Iron Curtain has descended

Speaking at Westminster College, in Fulton, Missouri, USA, on 5 March 1946, Winston Churchill was the first Western leader to state openly that he feared for the safety of his way of life in the face of the communist threat. The Soviets were particularly annoyed by his memorable phrase 'iron curtain'.

I have a strong admiration and regard for the valiant Russian people and for my wartime comrade, Marshal Stalin. There is deep sympathy and goodwill in Britain – and I doubt not here also – toward the peoples of all the Russias and a resolve to persevere through many differences and rebuffs in establishing lasting friendships.

It is my duty, however, ... to place before you certain facts about the present position in Europe.

In 1946, Europe was divided by an 'iron curtain'. It eventually included East Germany, west of Stettin.

From Stettin in the Baltic to Trieste in the Adriatic an iron curtain has descended across the Continent. Behind that line lie all the capitals of the ancient states of Central and Eastern Europe. Warsaw, Berlin, Prague, Vienna, Budapest, Belgrade, Bucharest and Sofia; all these famous cities and the populations around them ... are subject, in one form or another, not only to Soviet influence but to a very high and, in many cases, increasing measure of control from Moscow ...

In a great number of countries, far from the Russian frontiers and throughout the world, Communist fifth columns [activists operating in secret] are established and work in complete unity and absolute obedience to the directions they receive from the Communist centre.

Except in the British Commonwealth and in the United States where Communism is in its infancy, the Communist parties ... constitute a growing challenge and peril to Christian civilization.

# Cold War

By 1947 a 'Cold War' had broken out between US-led **democratic-capitalist** states, and USSR-led communist states: 'war' because there was dangerous tension, and 'cold' because there was no actual fighting between the **superpowers**. They came very close in 1962, when the Soviets attempted to base missiles in communist Cuba, only 145 km (90 miles) from the USA. Otherwise, they took opposing sides in conflicts. For example, in the Middle East war of 1967 the USSR supported the Arab nations while the USA backed Israel.

The two sides mistrusted each other deeply. The Soviets believed, probably correctly, that the USA wanted a democratic-capitalist world. The Americans believed, probably mistakenly, that the Soviets wanted to spread the communist revolution by force. In 1949, the **West** formed a self-defence pact, the North Atlantic Treaty Organization (NATO). The Soviet **bloc** responded with its own alliance, the Warsaw Pact (1955). Both agreements involved building up military forces that would act together to defend their side's interests.

The Cold War spilled over into non-military areas, such as sport (see page 24). It also fuelled a race between the USA and the Soviets to be the first into space. The USSR took the lead with the first satellite (1957) and the first manned space flight (1961), but the USA overtook them by landing the first person on the Moon (1969).

Gagarin in orbit, a Soviet **propaganda** triumph. The fact that it was the Russian, Yuri Gagarin, not an American, who became the first man in space (1961) was a great blow to US morale.

## Their fault, of course

The USA had **atomic bombs** by 1945 and the USSR by 1949, so there was always a real danger of the Cold War deteriorating into a nuclear conflict that might destroy all humanity. Simon Willis, born in England (1946) to a British mother and an American father, remembers the situation well.

We were brought up to hate the communists – 'Commies' we called them, both the Chinese and the Russians. With the Ruskies [Russians] it was the [atomic] bomb we feared most. My worst, recurring nightmare was nuclear war. I used to wake up in a sweat thinking that it had started and wondering where were we going to hide. I dreamed of those great mushroom clouds of A-bombs [atom bombs] going off somewhere in the distance, waiting for the blast, then the radiation.

At the time of the Cuban Missile Crisis it almost came true. I was at school then and our geography teacher, Mr. Parkinson, pinned up the front of the newspaper on his classroom door every day. That's how we saw the crisis develop, bit by bit.

The headlines talked about neither side being prepared to back down. We'd been told we'd have four minutes warning of an A-bomb attack – four minutes from the time the siren sounded to the moment the bomb went off – and my friends and I used to discuss what we'd do in those last four minutes. We joked about stuffing ourselves with ice cream, but really I think that deep down we were really scared. Quite a few of us really thought the world was going to end – blown to bits by the Commies.

It would be their fault, of course.

The closest the world has come to nuclear holocaust was the Cuban Missile Crisis of 1962. Here USS *Barry* (bottom) steams alongside the Soviet freighter *Ansonov* which was believed to be carrying parts of nuclear missiles to communist-governed Cuba, only 145 km (90 miles) from the US coast.

13

# Two Germanys

At the end of World War II Stalin was determined that German forces should never again invade Russia. He wanted not only to control the wealth and resources of eastern Germany, but to have the area as a buffer between the communist **East** and the **democratic-capitalist West**. Consequently, Germany was divided.

East Germany (German Democratic **Republic** or GDR), the region occupied by the **Red Army**, remained under communist rule. The Western powers established West Germany (Federal Republic of Germany or FRG) as a democratic-capitalist state. The capital city, Berlin, situated within the GDR, was split between communist (East Berlin) and US, British and French sectors (West Berlin).

After World War II, Berlin was divided into four sectors. The USSR controlled the eastern zone and the other **Allies** the western zones.

In the years following the division of Germany, it became clear that the communist **economic** system was less efficient at creating wealth than the capitalist system. Individuals seemed to work best for themselves, not the state. As a result, during the 1950s the economy of democratic-capitalist Western Europe advanced more swiftly than that of communist Eastern Europe.

In Germany the Soviets widened the East-West prosperity gap by plundering GDR wealth under the excuse of war reparations (the money paid by a defeated nation after a war). In June 1953 some 300,000 GDR workers rebelled against their communist government. The uprising was crushed by Soviet tanks. Citizens behind the Iron Curtain were beginning to see themselves as trapped within a Soviet empire.

## Disillusion

The GDR rebels of 1953 wanted a united Germany. They were also disillusioned because the communist 'workers' paradise' – a supposedly ideal world where everyone was equally well paid and cared for – had not materialized. The Soviet-backed GDR was more like the old Nazi **police state**. In this report the communist activist Cajo Brendel describes a demonstration by factory workers.

Stones against tanks. Unarmed East German citizens hurl stones at Soviet tanks sent in to protect government buildings during the 1953 uprising in the communist German Democratic Republic.

The workers of Henningsdorf stuck together and there were 12,000 of them. They marched arm in arm on a wide front. They came down the road which led from the north, still wearing their work clothes, and with their protective spectacles still hanging around their necks. Some wore shoes with wooden soles which echoed on the paving stones. The sound was amplified against the buildings of Millerstasze at Wassing, till it became an approaching storm which could sweep the Bolsh [the Bolsheviks were the communist group that had led the Russian Revolution] leadership clean out of the political scene.

It was pouring with rain when the workers of Henningsdorf left their factories. Soon they were completely soaked. But nothing could have held them back. There were women amongst them wearing light shoes, bought from the shop of the Organization of Commerce, . . . which weren't meant for heavy use like this. When their feet began to hurt, the women took off their shoes and continued barefoot. At no price were they going to be left behind. . . And as for the consequences of their action, no one had any precise idea of that.

15

# Hungary, 1956

As elsewhere in Eastern Europe, the **Red Army**'s occupation of Hungary in 1945 led inevitably to communist government. Life was made progressively harder for non-communists, and on 20 August 1949, the communist People's **Republic** of Hungary came into being.

Mátyás Rákosi, the leading communist and a strong supporter of Stalin, **purged** opponents in a reign of terror. However, following Stalin's death in 1953, the government of the USSR became less rigid. Press censorship was relaxed a little, for example, allowing people to read views that were not necessarily in full agreement with the communist party.

Young Hungarians raise their national flag over a toppled statue of Joseph Stalin, 1956. Despite its widespread popular support, the uprising was swiftly crushed by Warsaw Pact forces.

During this mood of '**destalinization**' (see page 20), the Hungarian government changed several times. Eventually, in 1955, Rákosi decided it was time to clamp down on anti-communist and anti-Soviet sentiments. This led to a violent anti-government and anti-Soviet revolution (23 October– 4 November 1956) that brought the moderate Imre Nagy in as prime minister. The new government begged the USA for help that did not come, and within days the revolt was brutally crushed. As in the GDR, Russian tanks rolled in and Soviet-style rule was re-established. Nagy was first replaced with the **hardline** minister Janos Kádár, then imprisoned and later executed. Kádár ruled the country as a **dictator** for the next 30 years.

## Nagy's last message

The Hungarian Revolution of 1956 was more anti-Russian than anti-communist. Prime Minister Imre Nagy said in his last speech to his people and the world at large (4 November 1956) that his main wish was for Hungary to be free to decide its own future, not have it dictated by Soviet Russia.

This fight is the fight for freedom by the Hungarian people against the Russian intervention, and it is possible that I shall only be able to stay at my post for one or two hours. The whole world will see how the Russian armed forces, contrary to all treaties and conventions, are crushing the resistance of the Hungarian people. They will also see how they are kidnapping the prime minister of a country which is a member of the United Nations, taking him from the capital, and therefore it cannot be doubted at all that this is the most brutal form of intervention.

I should like in these last moments to ask the leaders of the revolution, if they can, to leave the country. I ask that all that I have said in my broadcast, and what we have agreed on with the revolutionary leaders during meetings in Parliament, should be put in a memorandum, and the leaders should turn to all the peoples of the world for help and explain that today it is Hungary and tomorrow, or the day after tomorrow, it will be the turn of other countries, because the imperialism of Moscow does not know borders and is only trying to play for time.

Imre Nagy (1895-1958), the Hungarian prime minister who begged for US help to sustain his moderate government, 1956. No Western support came, and Nagy was later arrested and executed by pro-Soviet communists.

# The Prague Spring

The communists won 38 per cent of the vote in the Czech elections of May 1946. They were included in the government of President Benes and Prime Minister Masaryk that hoped to keep Czechoslovakia neutral, not aligned to **East** or **West**.

This policy collapsed in February 1948, when the communists, led by Klement Gottwald, formed a legitimate government. This was just the opening Gottwald needed – at the elections in May only communist party candidates were allowed to stand. **Purges** of opponents swiftly followed, making the Soviet-backed, intolerant regime secure.

Resentment at the government's **repression** and mismanagement of the **economy** grew until, in January 1968, a new First Secretary of the Communist Party, Alexander Dubcek, launched a programme of **reform**. During this 'Prague Spring' Dubcek attempted to make communist Czechoslovakia more open, fair and flexible. Yet again, fearing that greater freedom might eventually bring down the entire Soviet system, the Russians moved in with tanks and Warsaw Pact troops. Although there was no fighting, the Prague Spring came to an untimely end.

## The last free news

Cecile Køíová worked as a journalist for Radio Prague's American section, making broadcasts in English. She remembers vividly what happened to her on 21 August 1968, the day that Russian forces entered the Czech capital and ended its short-lived spring.

I was one of the lucky few who had managed to get into the radio building that day. There were barricades on the streets, even some of the bridges were barricaded. I went into the studio and read the news of the violent occupation of Czechoslovakia by Warsaw Pact troops, who no-one had invited, and handed over the microphone to a colleague from the French Section.

Suddenly the door to the studio flew open. In the doorway stood a soldier, his uniform covered in dust. He pointed a machine gun at me and said 'Von!' – which means 'Out!' in Russian.

I said I was already on my way out, thank you. And there ended nineteen years at Radio Prague. I'd just finished editing an interview with the American actress Shirley Temple. I'd recorded it the day before. It never went out. Soon afterwards I emigrated to the United States.

Russian troops march into Prague, the capital of Czechoslovakia, in 1968, bringing to an end the brief period of **liberal** rule known as the 'Prague Spring'.

19

# Fossilization in the USSR

**Marxists** believe communism to be the final and highest stage of human development. The USSR was in the stage before this – the **dictatorship** of the **proletariat** (see page 4). There could, therefore, be only one political party – the communist party – to form and lead the all-powerful government. The existence of just one party, which was sure that it knew all the answers, made change very difficult to bring about.

There was a general recognition after 1953 that Stalin's style of leadership had been faulty. He had been too harsh and had placed too much emphasis on the leader. His successor, Nikita Khrushchev who dominated the **Politburo** (1953-64), tried to undo some of Stalin's work in a policy known as **destalinization**.

The **cult** of the leader was played down, the rule of law more closely followed, and there was greater freedom for artists and writers. Nevertheless, Khrushchev was reluctant to make any dramatic changes for fear of undermining the 15-million-strong Communist Party. Under his cautious successor, Leonid Brezhnev (1964-82), the Soviet leadership became more and more tied to the army, upon whose power communism ultimately depended. Because the army was not interested in changing a system which benefited it so much, the USSR slowly **fossilized**.

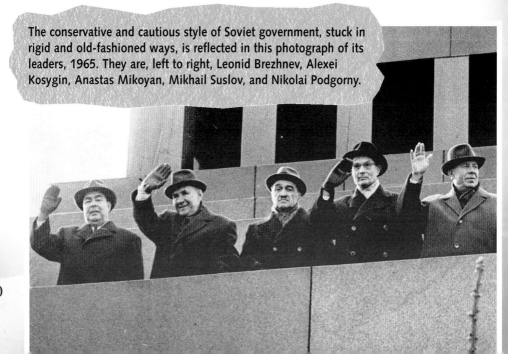

The conservative and cautious style of Soviet government, stuck in rigid and old-fashioned ways, is reflected in this photograph of its leaders, 1965. They are, left to right, Leonid Brezhnev, Alexei Kosygin, Anastas Mikoyan, Mikhail Suslov, and Nikolai Podgorny.

## I could not tell my classmates

Alexandra Osipova was born and brought up in the small town of Sudislavl, USSR. What she remembers most vividly about living under communism was the treatment of religion and church-going.

I think the church was very important to the Russian people. They wanted to be married and baptized there. They wanted to go to the church to say thank you to God when something good happened and to ask for help when things did not go right. But the communists would not allow this. After the Revolution [of 1917] many churches were closed or fell into ruin. The crosses fell off the top. Many priests – we called them 'fathers' – were killed. My cousin was a member of the Communist Party. He could not have his children baptized until 1990, when they were as old as eighteen, because if he had done so before and the communists had found out he would have lost his Communist Party [membership] card.

I remember when children from my school went to church at Christmas or Easter the teachers and local government workers and members of the Party stood round the church and took the names of all the people who came out after the service. The next day, at school, the headmaster read out these names in front of the whole school, saying how wrong they had been. That was very cruel. My grandmother took me to church but I could not tell even my classmates.

# Falling behind

One of the big problems of **capitalism**, according to communists and even many capitalists, is that the very rich often exploit (take advantage of) working people. To stop this happening communism outlawed private property, particularly large-scale businesses like farms and factories. All wealth-making, it declared, should be in the state's hands, and wealth distributed according to people's needs.

Soviet agriculture was organized in huge, state-owned **collective farms** on which all workers earned much the same wages. The system in factories and other enterprises was similar. This was called a command **economy**. The government set production targets for goods it decided were needed. During the 1950s, the system worked well and the economy grew by an average of about eleven per cent a year.

Women labourers help with the harvest on this Soviet collective farm in the 1930s. They are working for the common good. The USSR's leaders found that most people work less hard for the common good than they do for their own personal benefit.

Growth slowed in the 1960s and 70s. People had the basics of life – housing, food, pensions, health care – but at an increasingly lower standard than in the **West**. They also lacked the West's glittering array of **consumer goods**. Increasingly, Soviet citizens saw themselves as **repressed**, badly-dressed and dull neighbours of an altogether brighter and freer world on the other side of the Iron Curtain.

## Collective farming

Alexander Lyakin was an **icon** painter living on the Iskra collective farm near the city of Staritsa. He described how the communist system cut the link between work and reward. Without **incentive**, workers had little interest in their jobs.

The villages were dilapidated (broken down) and half of the houses boarded up and abandoned. The tractor repair station was littered with discarded parts and rusting agricultural machinery and so deep in mud that, even with boots on, it was difficult to walk there. In the fields, ragged clumps of uncut crops were still standing long after the harvest, sometimes partly submerged in snow.

Conversations among the collective farmers proceeded almost entirely in profanity (swearing), and the collective farmers seemed to have no interest in the outside world. Indolent (lazy) to a fault, they became active only when it was a matter of drinking or stealing.

The bosses reported for work promptly at 7:30 a.m. and decided on the day's work assignments. After about an hour, however, it was difficult to find them.

Shortly after 9 a.m. tractors appeared on the rutted roads. A sign on the machines read, DON'T TAKE PEOPLE, but this was ignored. Almost all of the tractors were pulling wagons that had several workers in them. There were many cases of wagons overturning and people being killed, especially when the driver was drunk.

It was soon possible to see small groups of people at work in various parts of the farm… In the fields, five or six women might be picking potatoes by hand while lying next to them was a man who was completely drunk.

# Two ways of life

In 1980 the rift between the **East** (communist) and the **West** (**democratic capitalist**) was as wide as ever. Afraid that the **Cold War** might burst into an all-out 'hot' or fighting war, each side had **stockpiles** of nuclear weapons sufficient to destroy the entire planet. In the Vietnam War, 1959-75, the USA had fought unsuccessfully to limit the advance of communism in Vietnam. Similarly, in 1979-89 the **Red Army** battled unsuccessfully in Afghanistan to uphold the communist government there.

The East-West divide seriously hampered the work of the United Nations (UN), an organization established in 1945 to promote peace and international co-operation. The UN's chief decision-making body, the Security Council, could only operate if everyone agreed on decisions. This was difficult because the USA and the USSR usually voted against each other. The same tit-for-tat arrangements affected sport, too. When the USA **boycotted** the 1980 Moscow Olympic Games in protest at the Soviet invasion of Afghanistan, the Soviets boycotted the 1984 Los Angeles Games in retaliation.

Both sides gave aid to favoured countries and political groups and engaged in a **propaganda** war. The West's biggest propaganda **ally** was Hollywood – one James Bond film, such as *From Russia With Love* (1963), probably did more harm to the image of the Soviet Union than any official propaganda.

The strain of the East-West hostility on the Soviet Union was immense. By 1975 its armed forces and related industries were absorbing some 40 per cent of its wealth. The situation was almost unsustainable.

Missiles on display at a military parade in Red Square, Moscow, 1987. Despite their stockpiles of nuclear weapons, both the USSR and the USA continued to pour huge sums of money into the **arms race**. This helped to weaken the Soviet **economy**.

## Reflecting the ideals of the West

In the USA, the victory of their ice hockey team over the USSR in the 1980 Lake Placid Winter Olympics (held before the US boycott) was seen as a triumph of Western sporting ideals over those of their communist opponents. This is part of Dave Kindred's report in the *Washington Post*.

When the ... young Americans beat the mighty Soviet Union — beat the very best hockey team on earth, 4-3 — the telephone rang with a call...

'President Carter said we made the American people very proud,' Brooks [the US coach] said after the United States' improbable victory ended the Soviets' 21-game winning streak in the Winter Olympics. 'He said we reflected the ideals of what the West and the USA stood for. He invited us to the White House [1600 Pennsylvania Avenue] for a couple of cases of Coke on Monday.'

... Who might imagine that the United States ... would set a thousand Old Glories [the US flag] waving in celebration? Only a fevered zealot could imagine that after this game the US players would rock their locker room with repeated renditions of 'God Bless America'.

Cold War on ice: the US ice hockey team celebrate victory over the USSR in the 1980 Winter Olympics.

'The crowd was an unbelievably big help to us,' the coach said. 'The fans displayed excellent sportsmanship, even though we have different ways of life and different government. There was no politics on behalf of the Russians and no politics by us. I don't think the fans were an ugly lot. They were positive.'

Including the fan at 1600 Pennsylvania Ave [President Carter].

# Poland's Solidarity

The first serious cracks within the Iron Curtain occurred in Poland. Many years of Russian domination had bred a fierce spirit of **nationalism** within the Polish people. This love of country was linked to an equally strong affection for the Roman Catholic Church.

Although firmly under Soviet control by 1945, Poland's Communist Party leaders (Wladyslaw Gomulka, 1956-70, and Edward Gierek, 1970-80) successfully argued that their country was a special case. Farms were not state-owned as in the USSR, the Church was tolerated, and Poles enjoyed greater liberty than their Iron Curtain neighbours.

During the 1970s, however, **economic** mismanagement and the lack of political freedom produced frequent unrest. This came to a head in 1980 with the formation of the **trade union** Solidarity, led by the popular Lech Walesa. Fearing armed Soviet intervention, in 1981 the government of Wojciech Jaruzelski clamped down on Solidarity and imprisoned its leaders. However, the anti-communist movement, boosted by visits from Pope John Paul II (who was born in Poland) in 1979, 1983 and 1987, could not be suppressed.

Polish students, some with their faces covered to avoid recognition by the secret police, march in support of the banned trade union Solidarity. The protest took place in 1987, during the visit of Pope John Paul II to his native Poland.

## An international symbol

The American magazine *Time* made Lech Walesa its 'Man of the Year' for 1981. In doing so, it revealed in emotional language its clear disapproval of the role played by the Soviet Union.

What had begun as Poland's year of liberty [1981] ended dramatically in violence, bloodshed and **repression**. The beleaguered government of General Wojciech Jaruzelski, . . . pressured by the furious Soviets, struck back in the classic Communist fashion. Its minions [servants] came for Walesa at 3 a.m. at his apartment in Gdansk . . . [and] hustled him aboard a flight to Warsaw and then held him in a government guesthouse… While the people slept, olive-drab tanks and armoured personnel carriers moved through the snow-filled streets to take up positions in cities and towns across the country.

At 6 a.m., Jaruzelski went on the radio . . . to announce that the nation was under **martial law**…The 'growing aggressiveness' of Solidarity's '**extremists**' in the midst of an acute economic crisis, said Jaruzelski, had forced him to make his repressive moves 'with a broken heart, with bitterness'.

…The crackdown had been harsh, fiercely and unexpectedly harsh. Thus, as 1981 came to a close, the courageous little electrician from Gdansk stood out not only as the heart and soul of Poland's battle with a corrupt Communist regime, but as an international symbol of the struggle for freedom and dignity … Lech Walesa is TIME's Man of the Year.

The voice of the people: with the eyes of the world upon him, Lech Walesa, the Polish shipyard worker turned politician, addresses a meeting of striking workers in Gdansk, 1980.

# Gorbachev

After Brezhnev's two elderly successors, Yuri Andropov (1982-84) and Constantin Chernenko (1984-85), leadership of the Soviet **Politburo** passed to the 54-year-old Mikhail Gorbachev. He recognized the USSR's serious **economic** problems and devised a three-part strategy to deal with them. First, Gorbachev pursued **détente** – more friendly **East-West** relations. This, he hoped, would reduce Soviet military expenditure as the risk of war would be reduced.

Second, he encouraged **glasnost** – open discussion – of the Soviet way and how it might be improved. For instance, writers were no longer to be punished for criticizing the Soviet system. The third policy was **perestroika** – restructuring the way the **economy** was managed. Farmers, for example, were to be allowed to sell small quantities of their produce directly to consumers instead of through state-owned shops.

With these policies Gorbachev hoped to get the most able party members into positions of authority instead of the most loyal (as had previously been the case). He was walking an impossible tightrope. *Glasnost* raised hopes of freedom that could not be fulfilled. *Perestroika* left the Soviet economy in an even worse state. *Détente* annoyed **conservatives** and the army. With **reformers** wanting more and **hardliners** wanting less, something had to give.

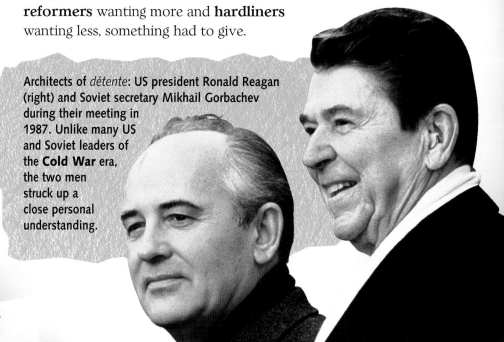

**Architects of** *détente*: US president Ronald Reagan (right) and Soviet secretary Mikhail Gorbachev during their meeting in 1987. Unlike many US and Soviet leaders of the **Cold War** era, the two men struck up a close personal understanding.

## It was a mess

Sacha Livtchak was a music student in the ancient and famous Russian city of Kostroma. Like many Russians, she greeted *perestroika* with mixed feelings.

*I remember it was a very difficult time. Before perestroika the discipline in Russia was very strong in the country – if people did wrong things, like stealing, they were punished very strictly. But after 1985 things began to change. There was so much corruption.* **Co-operatives** *started but they did not work unless they gave money to the people with power. The managers of factories sold everything they could – the machinery, the goods they made – just to put money in their pockets. They did not care about the people any more. After perestroika came, money was everything, and life got very corrupt and difficult.*

*When I was in music college we did not get grants or scholarships like students used to before Gorbachev. We had so little money we could not afford to buy even one little book. Our parents helped, of course, but it was difficult for them, too. Very often they did not get their wages. My boyfriend's parents did not get their wages for half a year. It was a very hard time. Do you know, culture suffered. It used to be very good under the communists because they were proud of it. After 1985, the good things (like classical music and having enough to eat) started to get bad, and the bad things (like not being able to say what you wanted) got better. It was a mess, really.*

# Economic disaster

Since Stalin's time the development of the Soviet **economy** had been organized in Five-Year Plans. The Twelfth Five-Year Plan (1985-90), under Gorbachev, attempted the impossible: to increase wealth by allowing more freedom for individuals while also keeping a tight control over what happened. Very simply, Gorbachev wanted the old system made more efficient by individual effort.

There was talk of workers participating more in the management of their businesses, of **co-operatives**, and of farmers **leasing** land to work on their own. Each idea ran into trouble with the Communist Party, which fought to keep its control. Meanwhile, the government spent more money than it had, and got into debt with foreign banks.

The results of these failures were catastrophic. National income rose by about 1 per cent a year to 1988, then fell by 12 per cent over 1989-90. By 1991 the average Soviet worker produced one third of their American counterpart and earned one fifth of the wages. Basic goods, even soap and shirts, were in short supply. As queues lengthened across the Soviet Union, the people had had enough.

Just as they used to do before the Revolution, hungry Muscovites queue for bread during the winter of 1986. Over the years that followed, the country's economic crisis deepened.

## Thank God I was born in the Soviet Union

Talking to David Satter, Moscow correspondent for the *Financial Times*, Vadim Pracht describes how **perestroika** and **glasnost** acted against each other. *Glasnost* let Soviet people see the world beyond the Iron Curtain and made them aware they were much worse off than people in the **West**.

I believed that Lenin was in general a great man, but now I don't think that any more...

I assumed that the United States was a country of enormous contrasts and that there was a small group that lived well and as far as simple people were concerned, I was convinced that they lived worse than we did. I thought, thank God I was born in the Soviet Union...

[Then] I went into the army and was isolated from *glasnost* and what was happening in the country. But when I came out in 1989, I began to read and was shocked by what I learned... I did not realize that for any innocent word, it was possible to land in a labour camp...

In the spring, there was a film about the Netherlands on the television... They showed a festival with flowers, streets where people did not have to spend all their time in queues, a country where a person did not have to worry constantly about where he would obtain a piece of meat or take a vacation with his family. There was a friendly atmosphere between people, people smiled at each other. Here if you smile at someone, you get an insult in return.

# Things fall apart

**Dissidents** had always criticized the Soviet system. Two of the more prominent were the scientist Andrei Sakharov, who was kept under house arrest from 1979 to 1986, and the writer Alexander Solzhenitsyn, who was deported (banished) from the USSR in 1974. *Glasnost* enabled millions to learn of their criticisms and, for the large part, share them.

Many people were in despair as the problems in the **economy** began to affect their lives. All across the USSR people began to complain. In Russia, **reformers** attacked the **repressive** and inefficient Soviet system. In other Soviet states, such as Lithuania, dissent merged with calls for independence from Russian rule.

People had a chance to express their feelings in the 1989 elections for the Soviet Congress (parliament). Thanks to *glasnost*, these elections were relatively free, and a range of anti-government candidates, communist and non-communist, were elected. Prominent among them was the popular radical reformer and opponent of Gorbachev, Boris Yeltsin.

Elsewhere in the USSR, opposition candidates from a range of parties were elected. By March 1990, when Russian troops tried, and failed, to stop Lithuania from becoming independent of the USSR, the Soviet Union was starting to fall apart.

The face of the future. Boris Yeltsin, opponent of the communist status quo, argues his case during the 1989 elections.

## Very little food

Having done compulsory military service in the Russian army in East Germany, Vittislav Oleksienko returned home to find a country that was on the point of collapse.

The prospect of freedom from Soviet rule has young Lithuanians dancing in the street in front of Vilnius Cathedral in March, 1989. About half a million people gathered for a peaceful anti-Soviet demonstration.

By 1990 corruption was everywhere. If you had a business, you had to pay what we called a 'roof' [protection money] to Mafia gangs or they would kill you or burn your place down. There were a lot of killings.

I remember three soldiers who used their authority to steal the radiators from a newly-built house. They then sold them and shared the money. When a senior officer got to hear of this, he was jealous and ordered the soldiers to seize the radiators again so he could sell them for himself. This happened but the men who took them were stopped by the military police, who beat them up and took the radiators to sell for themselves! That was normal.

There was very little food. Each person was given government coupons to buy things like sugar, flour, butter and vodka. The queues at the shops went on for hundreds of metres and you waited all day for things like flour and even bread. In the small towns and villages, everyone who could, kept a garden to grow vegetables and apples, and we went into the forest to pick berries and nuts to keep for the winter. Fresh food was too expensive to buy in the winter.

# Germany: the Wall comes down

In the years following the crushing of the 1953 revolt (see page 14), the GDR suffered as hundreds of thousands of its citizens fled across the border into West Berlin, the non-communist part of the divided city. To stop this happening, on 13 August 1961 the government of Walter Ulbricht erected a massive concrete wall across Berlin, sealing the **East-West** border. Although only part of the fortified border that divided the whole of Eastern Europe from the West, this Berlin Wall came to symbolize the Iron Curtain and communist **tyranny**.

Under Ulbricht's successor, Erich Honecker, the GDR's **economy** fared better than most communist states. Nevertheless, the regime remained **conservative**, rigid and **repressive**. When *glasnost* swept the USSR, Honecker stuck to his old ways. He was finally undermined by neighbouring Hungary, which opened its borders with Austria in the summer of 1989 and thereby provided an escape route to the West for GDR citizens.

Amid widespread anti-government demonstrations, Honecker resigned on 18 October 1989. Three weeks later (9 November) the **checkpoints** across Berlin were opened and delighted crowds began dismantling the wall with their bare hands. A year later the communist GDR ceased to exist as Germany was reunited into a single **democratic-capitalist** state.

## Come on, shoot!
Ger Tillekens worked in a hospital in West Berlin during the summer of 1973. From his apartment he had a clear view of the infamous Berlin Wall that divided the city in two.

From above . . . the Wall . . . proved to be not just a stone wall but a real barricade, filled with concrete road blocks, rolls of barbed wire and Todesstreifen, the sand stripes between the walls. At night the spotlights went on and we observed the Vopos [East German guards] making their rounds. . . Soon, however, we got used to it. . . Until, one night, we were awakened by the snarling sound of machine guns . . . and suddenly it all became very real.

The next morning we learned that a man had tried to climb the Wall, but was shot while crossing the sand stripes and had been left there, bleeding to death. It caused a real uproar with people gathering from all around . . . and I still have a vivid memory of a Berliner, standing on one of the wooden watch towers near the Wall, his arms spread wide in a dramatic gesture, shouting 'Schiess denn!' (Come on, shoot!) to the guards on the other side. . .

Within the pessimism about what had happened, though, there was always some sort of hopeful belief, mixed with anger . . . that in time the Wall would and should have to fall – though few people really thought they would live to see it happen.

A crane and bulldozer finally dismantle the Berlin Wall, the symbol of communist repression in post-war Europe, 12 November 1989.

# Central Europe: eager for capitalist democracy

Throughout Central Europe, **nationalism** and **economic** difficulties combined with the new freedom to speak out (*glasnost*) to produce unstoppable popular revolts. Gorbachev dared not use force for fear that the troops would not obey him when Poland elected a non-communist prime minister in 1989. Thereafter, despite economic hardship, Poland's **capitalist democracy** thrived.

Freely elected at last: the new Polish prime minister, Tadeusz Mazowiecki, joins with Lech Walesa (right) to celebrate the triumph of liberal democracy.

Gustav Husák guided Czechoslovakia with a moderate hand after the suppression of the 1968 Prague Spring (see page 18). Opposition centred around Václav Havel, who helped organize a petition known as Charter '77. This drew attention to the government's **human rights** abuses. With *glasnost* the opposition gained confidence and called a general strike in November 1989. Husák's power melted away and he was replaced by the opposition in what the Czechs called the '**Velvet Revolution**'. Four years later (1993), Czechoslovakia chose to divide peacefully into the Czech and Slovak **Republics**.

After the 1956 revolt (see page 16), Hungary's communist leader János Kádár gradually relaxed his **hardline** stance. Some private farms were permitted, for example. With the coming of *glasnost* it became possible to criticize the government, and in 1987 an opposition party (the MDF) was formed. Kádár resigned in 1988, and in 1990, Hungary held free elections which were won by the MDF.

## Soldier of the Velvet Revolution

Czechoslovakia's 'Velvet Revolution' was remarkable for its lack of violence, almost as if the entire country had been waiting for it to happen. Michal Lobkowicz, who went on to serve in the Czech parliament and as defence minister, remembers those happy, heady days.

*I think I was in quite a similar position to many other Czechs. I was young when the big change came in '89. And it seemed to be – and was – a big challenge for all of us. And a lot of us were feeling motivated to enter public life and to somehow help the country to move ahead… So I think it was a really challenging time. All of us felt that there was a need for action and that we had to take part in it. I was – as I always call it – a soldier of the revolution… I was distributing materials and I was participating in all the demonstrations and so on. So I was just one of hundreds of thousands of people who were individually protesting against the regime…*

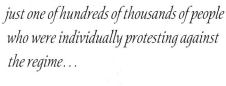

Delighted students, ringing bells and waving posters of their outstanding **dissident** leader Václav Havel, celebrate Czechoslovakia's Velvet Revolution (winter 1989).

*Then during the revolution itself, in November, I was part of a very numerous team – there were a lot of people – and we were travelling all around the country and meeting people. Basically there were big meetings in theatres and in factories. And we were going there and telling people what we were a part of, and that it was good … and that we wanted the country to become a normal western-type country. So we were acting like 'agents', travelling a lot around the country and trying to persuade the people that what was going on was good.*

# South-eastern Europe: bloody transition

The communist states of south-east Europe found the change from strict, **dictatorial** government to **democracy** difficult to make. Their people had little or no experience of democracy. Popular demonstrations achieved the resignation of the Bulgarian communist leader Todor Zhivkov on 9 November 1989, but his party remained intact. Following a popular uprising against his personal rule, the Romanian communist dictator Nicolae Ceausescu was executed on Christmas Day 1989. The country's new leader, Ion Iliescu, although confirmed in his post by popular election, maintained the **secret police** and several other unpleasant features of Ceausescu's dictatorship.

Albania was ruled by Enver Hoxha, and **allied** itself with communist China rather than the USSR. It was the last Stalinist state in Europe. When Hoxha died in 1985, the new leader, Ramiz Alia made opposition legal. Free elections were held in 1992, and won by the Democratic Party of Albania. However, the country remained desperately poor.

Yugoslavia was a country of diverse racial and religious groups, and when communist rule collapsed, the country broke apart. In 1991 the region of Slovenia declared itself an independent state. Croatia, Macedonia and Bosnia-Herzegovina soon followed, leaving only Serbia and Montenegro of the original Yugoslavia. The break-up was accompanied by bitter and bloody fighting, made much worse by long-standing religious and racial hatreds. It was all a far cry from the joyful celebrations in Berlin.

The collapse of communism brought disaster as well as joy. This elderly Bosnian visits the grave of his wife who had been pointlessly shot dead during the civil war that accompanied the break-up of communist Yugoslavia.

# The Times

### 27 December 1989

The **interim Government** in Romania appointed a President and Prime Minister yesterday as chilling details emerged about the execution by firing squad of former President Ceausescu and his wife Elena.

The couple's last words were: 'We want to die together,' and they were shot side by side without being blindfolded.

An army captain . . . said that several hundred soldiers had attended the couple's trial and that every one of them had volunteered to join the firing squad…

Captain Mihai Lupoi, who was at the trial, gave the first details of the proceedings . . . as Romanian television showed pictures of the bodies.

The corpse of Romania's communist dictator Nicolae Ceausescu who was shot dead on Christmas Day 1989 after only a brief trial. The overthrow of communism in Romania involved considerable loss of life as some of Ceausescu's security forces put up stiff resistance.

They were slumped against the base of a bullet-pocked wall in a military barracks, confirming beyond reasonable doubt that the former dictator and his wife had been executed… The charges against him and his wife were read in a voice-over. These included genocide of 60,000 people, destruction of the **economy**, issuing of criminal orders to the Army and depositing more than $1 billion (£600 million) in foreign banks.

The trial lasted for two hours and the execution took place at 4 p.m. on Christmas Day. According to Captain Lupoi, the Ceausescus refused to recognize the authority of the court, and Mrs Ceausescu protested to the soldiers: 'I am like a mother to you.'

# Russia: Yeltsin and the coup

Meanwhile, Gorbachev had lost control of the revolution he had started. In May 1990, Boris Yeltsin was elected chairman of the Russian **Supreme Soviet**. As leader of the country's parliament, he was to all intents and purposes, prime minister and undisputed leader of the radical **reformers**.

With shortages and price rises fanning popular discontent, Gorbachev's power to get things done dwindled. The Party was scorned everywhere and the USSR itself was disintegrating. Terrified at where it might end, in August 1991 a group of **conservative** communists, military commanders, and KGB (**secret police**) officers

attempted a **coup**. They seized Gorbachev in his country house and announced that he had resigned.

Still president but no longer with the people's support: Mikhail Gorbachev speaks to TV reporters after the failure of the Russian coup, August 1991.

Immediately, Yeltsin went into action to save the reforms, appealing to people to defy the tanks and soldiers sent to take control of Moscow's parliament building. Faced with vigorous popular opposition in the capital and St. Petersburg, the badly-organized coup collapsed. Gorbachev's day was over – he resigned on Christmas Day 1991. The USSR's **republics** were already deciding their own futures. Finally, at midnight on 31 December 1991, laws took effect that meant the Soviet Union had ceased to exist.

### Read and pass on to others

On hearing of the coup, Yeltsin hurried to the White House (the Russian parliament building in Moscow) and issued this statement calling on the citizens to join him in saving true **democracy**. Within hours, the building was surrounded by volunteers.

**To the Citizens of Russia –
19 August 1991**

On the night of 18 to 19 August 1991 the legally elected president of the country was removed from power. Whatever reasons might be given to justify this removal, we are dealing with a right-wing, **reactionary** and anti-constitutional coup.

Notwithstanding all the trials and difficulties the people of our country are experiencing, the democratic process in the country is becoming ever deeper and is becoming irreversible. The peoples of Russia are becoming masters of their own fate...

We have always considered the use of force to solve political and economic problems is unacceptable. It discredits the USSR in the eyes of the world and ... [returns] us to the **Cold War** era of isolation of the Soviet Union from the international community...

The man who saved the state. Boris Yeltsin, clasping the hand of a tank driver who had been sent to oust him, waves to crowds of supporters in front of the Russian parliament building, August 1991. Yeltsin's swift action had rallied the support of the people against the attempted coup – and made him the most popular man in the land.

We are absolutely convinced that our compatriots will not allow the arbitrary rule and lawlessness of these putschists [coup organizers], men with neither shame nor conscience, to become firmly established. We appeal to the troops to demonstrate a sense of civic duty and not to take part in this reactionary coup.

We call for a general strike until such time as these demands are met...

Read and pass on to others.

# The USSR: liberation

As the fifteen-state USSR went out of existence, a new organization, the Commonwealth of Independent States (CIS), came into being. This was a free association of Russia and eleven of the former Soviet **republics** (the Baltic States refused to join) to co-ordinate policies on matters such as **economics**, defence, and environmental protection. Its benefits were not immediately obvious.

Communism was not necessarily replaced by **democratic capitalism**, nor did its collapse always bring a better life for ex-Soviet citizens. Roughly speaking, newly independent states in the west benefited more than those further east (see pages 44-45). After initial anxieties and difficulties, the Baltic states of Estonia, Latvia and Lithuania developed fairly stable Western-style democratic systems and sought membership of the European Union.

(see pages 44-45).

**Mixed reception**
Mikhailo Boichyshyn, a leader of Rukh, the Ukrainian opposition movement, had difficulty persuading people in eastern Ukraine to join him in 1990. His experience reminds us that communism and the USSR were by no means universally hated.

Sandwiched between Russia and the **West**, Belarus struggled to develop a free and democratic system of government. Further south, the small, landlocked state of Moldova had trouble establishing a national identity. This was less of a problem for their much larger neighbour Ukraine. Nevertheless, the country was beset by economic difficulties, political unrest, and deep-rooted corruption.

Civil war in Moldova, 1992. Supporters of the break-away Transdnestr Republic in action against Moldavian forces.

A Ukrainian woman makes her views known at an independence rally in 1991. She, for one, wants change. Her poster reads "And you!? Will you return to the USSR prison cell?"

Everywhere he went Boichyshyn encountered puzzlement or hostility.

In Ternopol, [he] took part in the ceremonial reburial of the victims of a Stalin-era execution squad, and after the reinterment [reburial], he spoke about the history of political terror in the Ukraine. During most of the speech, the audience listened respectfully, but when he said it was Lenin who gave the first orders for shooting priests, there were shouts of protest and people in the crowd began saying it was all lies…

In Poltava … Boichyshyn led the demonstrators to a nearby park, where he argued that the Ukraine would be able to control its own fate only under conditions of independence…

Finally, a woman in the crowd shouted, 'I agree that the Ukraine should be independent, but you can't come out this way against Lenin, against the red flag and all that we fought for in the Second World War.'

… In Donetsk, Rukh activists, including Boichyshyn, went from mine to mine handing out leaflets and literature. Almost nowhere were they well received … 'It's all the same to us what language [Russian or Ukrainian] we speak,' one miner told Boichyshyn, 'as long as there is sausage.'

Boichyshyn referred to the people who expressed these views as 'sausage people'.

# The USSR: new tyranny

For a majority of the inhabitants in the southern and eastern
**republics** of the former USSR, life was probably worse than it had
been under communism. Communism had at least offered most
Soviet citizens a degree of security and a guarantee of certain basic
needs such as food, housing and elementary medical care. After 1991
even these were uncertain in most ex-Soviet republics. The people
had no experience of **democracy**, nor did they know how to operate
free-market **capitalism**. As a result, power usually passed to
gang-leaders and **warlords**. Resources were sometimes drained by
war, too. Chechnya fought a long and vicious war of independence
with Russia. Georgia and other states were also engaged in armed
conflict with breakaway movements.

Corruption and crime thrived under **tyrannical** governments. The
situation was probably worst in Uzbekistan, Kazakhstan, Tajikistan,
and Turkmenistan. The **dictatorship** of Turkmenistan by the former
communist official President Niyazov – 'Great Hero of the Nation and
Father of all Turkmen' – was most distasteful. Niyazov was such a
**megalomaniac** that he replaced the word for 'bread' with his
mother's name and abolished old age. His idiotic tyranny made
communist rule seem almost pleasant.

Kyrgyzstan, the state most keen for independence,
gladly accepted capitalist democracy and was a
clear exception to the general **mayhem**.

No choice for the
Chechens. A mother
and child pass a beggar
in the ruined centre of
Grozny, the capital of
Chechnya, 1995. The
Russians quashed the
region's independence
movement in a long
and bloody civil war.

## Caught in the cross-fire

Chechnya declared itself independent of Russia in 1991. Russia rejected the move as illegal and likely to inspire similar independence bids elsewhere. This sparked years of bitter fighting marked by atrocities on both sides in which many innocent people were killed. This account tells how the terrified people of Alkhan-Yurt, near the Chechen capital Grozny, reacted when Chechen **guerillas** came to their village.

The residents of Alkhan-Yurt did not invite Chechen fighters to their town and did everything within their powers to get the fighters to leave the village. Many residents of Alkhan-Yurt expressed their anger toward the Chechen fighters.

The fighters were not . . . defending us but were there only out of their own interests. Every street of our village is visible from Sunzhan ridge [where the Russian firing positions were located]. Our village is not made for defence, but the fighters came anyway. Near the cemetery, there is a stand of woods, and there they dug their trenches. We . . . demanded that they leave, but they told us to leave and threatened to shoot.

On November 16, Haji Vakha Muradov and three other respected elders from the village attempted to meet with the fighters to convince them to leave the village: "I begged them on behalf of the village, 'Please leave our village, this is not a place for you to fight. The whole village will be on your side, just please leave.'" According to Muradov, the commander of the Chechen fighters replied that they would not leave, and reportedly said, "We cannot retreat from Russian soldiers. We are not going to hand the city [Grozny] over to them. We are not going to let the soldiers get to the city through this village. We are going to fight."

# Change and resistance around the world

In 1980, communism was spread around the world and seemed unassailable. Within a few years, however, Cuba (see below), North Korea, and China (see pages 48-49) were the only remaining communist states. Elsewhere, communist movements and parties had shrivelled in the fresh **democratic-capitalist** breeze blowing from Moscow. The end of the **Cold War** gave the United Nations a new lease of life (see page 24), while cuts in military spending freed up money and people to work for more beneficial purposes – the so called 'peace dividend'.

The European Union prepared to expand into Eastern Europe. Even bigger changes took place in Southern Africa. Here, before 1989, the African National Congress (ANC), opponents of South Africa's all-white **apartheid** regime, had been labelled communist by the regime. Consequently, the **West** had given almost unspoken support to the whites.

With the ending of the Cold War the accusation that the ANC was backed by communists was no longer relevant, so Western support was withdrawn and the apartheid regime ended. In neighbouring Mozambique, Angola and Namibia the battle between communism and democratic capitalism had been fought out in bitter civil wars in which the opposing factions were funded by the USSR (often via Cuba) and the West. These conflicts, too, came to an end. Almost everywhere, it seemed, the cause of democratic capitalism was triumphant.

### We will never change – because we are right
The communist regime on the island of Cuba, led by Fidel Castro and long backed by the USSR, remained almost untouched by the momentous changes going on around it. Speaking in 1995, Castro explained why he thought communism had survived in his country.

I'm still being left out of the dinners and the receptions [in the USA], as if nothing had changed, as if we were still in the days of the Cold War. But if others have not changed, we will not change either ... we will never change, because we are right...

I think our people have carried out their ideals. Millions of people have been taken care of by our doctors in Africa, in Latin America, and other parts of the world. Thousands of Cuban teachers and professors have trained technicians.

Cuba ... is the country ... that has raised life expectancy to almost 76 years, that has reduced infant mortality from 60 deaths per 1000 live births to less than 10, and in doing so has saved the lives of hundreds of thousands of children.

We have the highest number of teachers and professors per capita in the world. We have the highest percentage of doctors in the world.

We have done something more than that... Over 2000 Cubans gave their lives in internationalist missions, fighting **colonialism**. If there is something that makes us proud, it is the 15 years that we fought against South Africa, against racism and apartheid.

Fidel Castro, the Cuban dictator who resolutely refused to accept the changes that swept through the communist world at the end of the 20th century.

47

# China's market communism

After the collapse of the Soviet Union, China was by far the largest remaining communist state. Although the Chinese Communist Party (CCP) played much the same role as the Soviet Communist Party had done, Chinese communism was different.

The government took over agriculture and industry after Mao Zedong's victory in 1949 (see page 8). In 1966, faced with mounting criticism, Mao launched a period of fanatical communist **mayhem** known as the Cultural Revolution. Gangs of young Red Guards terrorized the country, attacking anyone and anything that seemed even vaguely non-communist. The revolution ended with Mao's death in 1976, and, under the more moderate leadership of Deng Xiaoping, China altered course.

Two features marked the new policy. First, the CCP maintained its strict, absolute rule. The worst example of this was the shocking massacre of large numbers of pro-**democracy** protestors in Beijing's Tiananmen Square in 1989. Second, communist **economics** was gradually abandoned in favour of free-market (**capitalist**) principles. While this produced remarkable growth rates (about 10 per cent a year), especially in China's south-eastern provinces, it led to a widening gap between the new rich and the bulk of the population.

One man's statement: Chinese tanks sent to suppress the pro-democracy rally in Beijing, 1989, halt before a lone protester. The tanks drove round the man, who was unharmed – unlike the many fellow protestors later killed and wounded in Tiananmen Square.

## Freedom of information

Modern technology, such as the Internet and satellite television, has made it increasingly hard for **repressive** regimes to control people's access to information. The Chinese authorities, however, still tried. Bobson Wong, on the Digital Freedom Network, cites the following case.

### Chinese student detained for publishing articles online

The New York-based China Labor Watch said earlier this week that Liu Di, a 22-year-old psychology student at Beijing Normal University, was detained on November 7 while on campus. Police later searched her family's apartment and took away her family's computer and other items.

Liu Di was living with her grandmother, Liu Heng, ... a retired People's Daily reporter ... [and] one of the few intellectuals labeled an 'incorrigible rightist' for her outspoken criticism of the Communist Party in 1957...

The free-market economy has brought capitalist glitz to places like Nanjing Road, Shanghai, pictured here in 2002, but the government is less happy with the freedom offered by the Internet.

Li Qiang, executive director of China Labor Watch, said that Liu [Di] had published several articles on the Xici online bulletin board that criticized the government's restrictions on the Internet.

Using the name 'Stainless Steel Mouse,' one of Liu's articles expressed sympathy for Huang Qi, a webmaster who was jailed in June 2000 after ... an online bulletin board for missing persons that he used to run, published articles relating to several taboo topics, including the 1989 Tiananmen Square pro-democracy demonstrations...

Liu also criticized the recent shutdown of Internet cafés. On June 16, after a fire in an unlicensed cybercafé in Beijing ... authorities closed all Internet cafés in the city ... Of the 2400 cafés that were in business before the fire, only a handful have reopened, with filtering software and monitoring tools in place...

Liu's current location is unknown.

# What have we learnt from the collapse of communism?

Many Westerners believe communism collapsed because it was based on a false view of human nature. As events in the Soviet Union showed, they say, we are imperfect, competitive creatures. Only **democracy** controls our quest for power and only **capitalism** harnesses our thirst for gain. Communists reply that Soviet failure does not make communism itself invalid.

Why did Soviet communism fall when it did? The final collapse of the Soviet **economy** after years of decline was important, as was Gorbachev's decision to allow free speech but not to listen to what was said. The USA and its

### My Soviet memories
When the first enthusiasm of liberty had died down, many citizens of the former USSR began to find that life under capitalism was much tougher than they had expected. Some, like this anonymous student, were soon longing for a return of the 'good old days'.

**allies** played their part, too, by luring the USSR into an unequal struggle for power and prosperity that eventually bankrupted it.

Is the post-Soviet world a better place? The poverty-stricken people of Turkmenistan and many other parts of the former USSR would say not. Others are uneasy at world domination by a single **superpower**, the USA. Then there are those, including some religious groups, unhappy at what they see as the triumph of capitalism and materialism.

Possibly, we may find that the collapse of Soviet communism created as many problems as it solved.

Capitalism does not equal plenty for all, at least not in the short run – Muscovites queue for low-priced milk, 1998.

All the trimmings of the Western world for these Muscovites in a McDonald's restaurant, 1996. This would have been unthinkable under communism.

My life was pretty clear, without any major worries, and all roads in life were open for me when I grew up. It was not a question of whenever you can afford it to go to university – it was simply a matter of you doing your best at school and knowing what you want to become.

I had an extremely happy childhood. Not rich or posh or anything like that, but that is not what makes you happy. I had a very loving and caring family around me; I had plenty of interesting books, I have travelled more than any of my friends – every year several times with my mother, all around the USSR, and it was an enormous country!

The life was sometimes a bit boring, maybe a bit predictable, but we never knew what it is like to worry about your tomorrow. . .

In 1984 I entered the prestigious Moscow State Institute for History and Archival Science. . . The new life, the five most interesting and most happy years in my life, had begun. Little did I know that the dark clouds were coming together over my country, my way of life and everything I cared about, and that my life will never be the way I wanted it to be, after that.

# Timeline

1867 Marx publishes first volume of key communist text, *Das Kapital*
1917 Communist Revolution in Russia
1922 USSR established
1924 Lenin dies
1928 Stalin in power
1939 Outbreak of World War II in Europe
1941 June: German attack on USSR; Britain and USSR **allied**
Dec: Japanese attack on Pearl Harbor
USA enters the war as an ally of USSR
1945 February: Churchill, Roosevelt and Stalin meet at Yalta
May: war in Europe ends. Eastern Germany under Soviet control
1946 Yugoslavia, Albania and Bulgaria become communist states
March: Churchill's 'Iron Curtain' speech marks beginning of **Cold War**
1947 Poland becomes communist state; USA starts giving **economic** aid to Western Europe (Marshall Plan)
1948 Romania and Czechoslovakia become communist states
1949 March: NATO founded
August: Hungary becomes communist state
Mao Zedong declares People's Republic of China (communist)
1953 March: death of Stalin
Khrushchev leader of USSR (to 1971)
June: anti-government rebellion in East Germany
1955 May: Warsaw Pact established
1956 Anti-communist rebellion in Hungary
1957 October: Soviets launch first Earth-orbiting satellite
1958 January: USA launches its first satellite
1961 April: Soviet cosmonaut Yuri Gagarin first man in space
August: Berlin Wall erected
1962 October: Cuban Missile Crisis
1964 Brezhnev leader of the USSR (to 1982)
Return to rigid communist principles
Soviet **economy** slowing down
1968 August: forces of the Warsaw Pact crush Prague Spring
1974 Solzhenitsyn exiled from USSR
Death of Mao Zedong. Start of liberalization of the Chinese economy
Sakharov under house arrest (to 1986)

Pope John Paul II visits Poland
1980 USA and several other **Western** states boycott Moscow Olympics
September: Solidarity, an independent **trade union**, formed in Poland
1981 Polish trade union Solidarity outlawed
1982 Andropov leader of the USSR (to 1984)
USA and USSR discuss arms reduction
1984 Warsaw Pact countries boycott Los Angeles Olympics
1985 Gorbachev leader of the USSR (to 1991). Extensive talks with US President Reagan on arms reduction
Policies of **glasnost** and **perestroika** announced
1986 Sakharov released
USSR permits private enterprise
1987 MDF opposition movement formed in Hungary
Further arms reductions talks
1988 Gorbachev talks of 'democratization' and gets free elections for a new assembly, the Congress of People's Deputies
May: Hungarian hard-line communist leadership resigns
August: Pro-Solidarity strikes in Poland
1989 Widespread shortages in USSR
Soviet troops leave Afghanistan
Free elections to Soviet Congress return many anti-government candidates, including Yeltsin
November: Berlin Wall comes down
**Velvet Revolution** in Czechoslovakia
Bulgarian communist leadership resigns
December: Romanian communist regime falls
1990 March: Lithuania declares itself independent
East Germans vote for unification with West Germany
May: Yeltsin Russian prime minister
October: Germany reunited
December: Walesa elected president of Poland
1991 Slovenia declares itself independent from Yugoslavia
July: USA and USSR sign START arms reduction treaty
August: Reactionary coup in Russia fails
December: Gorbachev resigns
USSR ceases to exist

# Find out more

## Books & websites

*Cold War*, Jeremy Isaacs & Taylor Downing, (Bantam, 1998)
*Leading Lives: Joseph Stalin*, David Downing, (Heinemann Library, 2001)
*Political and Economic Systems: Communism*, Richard Tames, (Heinemann Library, 2002)
*Troubled World: Wars of Former Yugoslavia*, David Taylor, (Heinemann Library, 2001)
*Turning Points in History: The Cuban Missile Crisis*, Fergus Fleming, (Heinemann Library, 2001)
*20th Century Perspectives: The Cold War*, David Taylor, (Heinemann Library, 2001)
*20th Century Perspectives: The Russian Revolution*, Tony Allan, (Heinemann Library, 2002)

http://news.bbc.co.uk/hi/english/static/special_report/1999/09/99/iron_curtain

http://wwics.si.edu

http://www.bbc.co.uk/history/war/coldwar/soviet_end_01.shtml

http://www.cnn.com/SPECIALS/cold.war

http://www.coldwar.net

http://www.coldwar.org/index.html

http://www.dailysoft.com/berlinwall

http://www.fas.org/man/dod-101/ops/docs/coldwar_timeline.htm

http://www.fordham.edu/halsall/mod/modsbook46.html

# List of primary sources

The author and publisher gratefully acknowledge the following publications and websites from which written sources in the book are drawn. In some cases the wording or sentence structure has been simplified to make the material more appropriate for a school readership.

Page 9 Brigadier J.G. Smyth, *Daily Sketch*, 8 May 1945
Page 11 Winston Churchill, speech at Westminster College, Fulton, Missouri, 5 March 1946
Page 13 Simon Willis, personal interview with the author, April 2003
Page 15 Cajo Brendel, pamphlet first published in Dutch, July 1953, cited on
   www.geocities.com/cordobakaf/brendel_germany.html
Page 17 Imre Nagy, last speech, 4 November 1956
Page 19 Cecile Køiová, cited on Prague Radio website:
   www.radio.cz/en/html/65_praguespring.html
Page 21 Alexandra Osipova, personal interview with the author, May 2003
Page 23 Alexander Lyakin, cited in David Satter, *Age of Delirium: The Decline and Fall of the Soviet Union*, Yale University Press, 2001
Page 25 Dave Kindred, *Washington Post*, 23 February 1980
Page 27 Thomas A. Sancton, *Time* magazine, 4 January 1982
Page 29 Sacha Livtchak, personal interview with the author, May 2003

Page 31 Vadim Pracht, cited in David Satter, *Age of Delirium: The Decline and Fall of the Soviet Union*, Yale University Press, 2001

Page 33 Vittislav Oleksienko, personal interview with the author, May 2003

Page 35 Ger Tillekens, Berlin Wall Online, cited on www.dailysoft.com/berlinwall/memories/memories_04.html

Page 37 Radio Prague interview cited on http://www.radio.cz/en/article/36168

Page 39 Michael Hornsby, *The Times*, 27 December 1989

Page 41 Boris Yeltsin, statement issued in Moscow, 19 August 1991

Page 43 Mikhailo Boichyshyn, cited in David Satter, *Age of Delirium: The Decline and Fall of the Soviet Union*, Yale University Press, 2001

Page 45 Cited on www.russia.com/forums/showthread.php3?threadid=5312&pagenumber=5

Page 47 Fidel Castro, a talk in Harlem, 22 October, 1995 cited in *Workers World*, 2 November, 1995, copyright Workers World Service

Page 49 Bobson Wong, Digital Freedom Network, 10 December 2002, cited on www.oneworld.net

Page 51 Anonymous Russian student, cited on http://nuance.dhs.org/lbo-talk/0205/2137.html

# Glossary

**Allies, the**   Western powers and the USSR who fought together in World War II

**ally**   state, organization or person that supports another

**apartheid**   South Africa's previous policy of separating the white and black populations, giving less favourable opportunities to the latter

**arms race**   name given to the competitive building of more and more weapons by the USA and USSR

**atomic bomb**   earliest form of nuclear bomb

**bloc**   group of states

**boycott**   to refuse to attend or take part in

**capitalism**   economic system based on the free manufacture, buying and selling of all goods

**checkpoint**   road block where papers are checked

**Cold War**   period of East-West tension, 1946-89, that stopped short of a hot (fighting) war

**collective farm**   state-owned farm

**colonialism**   act of taking over and ruling other people's territories, usually overseas

**conservative**   cautious about change

**consumer goods**   non-essential goods, such as cars and washing machines

**co-operative**   an enterprise owned and controlled by the people who work in it

**coup**   attempt to seize power suddenly and by force

**cult**   worship of a person

**democracy**   a system of government in which the governed – the people – periodically choose their governors in free elections. Genuinely democratic states uphold human rights and freedoms

**destalinization**   change from a dictatorial style of government like that of Joseph Stalin

**détente**   greater understanding and friendship

**dictatorship**   government by an all-powerful ruler (dictator) or ruling group

**dissident**   one who strongly objects to a government

**East** Eastern Europe and the USSR

**economics** financial aspects, including money production, distribution and sale of goods and services

**economy** all production, distribution and sale of goods and services

**extremists** fanatical supporters

**feudalism** system in which land and protection are given in exchange for work and military service

**fossilize** become antiquated and unable to change

**free enterprise** system in which private business operates in competition and largely free of state control

*glasnost* open-speaking

**guerillas** group of unofficial fighters

**hardliners** those unwilling to change

**human rights** basic rights, e.g. freedom of speech, that should belong to every person

**icon** small religious painting

**incentive** the promise of a reward

**interim government** temporary, unelected government

**leasing** renting

**liberal** willing to change

**martial law** government by the army

**Marxism** political and economic system devised by Karl Marx

**mayhem** violent chaos

**megalomaniac** someone who believes themselves to be all-powerful and who seeks all power

**nationalism** vigorous enthusiasm for one's country

**objectively** unaffected by feelings or opinions

*perestroika* restructuring of the communist system attempted in the USSR 1985-90

**philosopher** one who considers the deeper meaning of things in life

**police state** state where the people are controlled by political (often secret) police

**Politburo** the chief Soviet decision-making committee

**proletariat** working class

**propaganda** information slanted to support one side or blacken another

**purge** forcibly remove unwanted people, sometimes by killing them

**reactionary** unwilling to accept any change

**Red Army** army of the USSR

**reformers** those who seek improvement through change

**repression** holding down of

**republic** state with elected leadership, without a king or queen

**secret police** police force operating in secret for political purposes

**socialist** *either* another word for communist, *or* a moderate and democratic system of government aiming at public ownership of the means of production, and equality in society. Within the USSR 'communist' and 'socialist' were interchangeable. Elsewhere, particularly in Western Europe, 'socialist' generally means a moderate and democratic system of government.

**stockpile** large collection of something, usually arms

**superpower** major world power

**Supreme Soviet** Soviet parliament abolished in 1990

**trade union** group of workers who get together to protect or extend their interests

**tyranny** cruel use of authority

**Velvet Revolution** Czechoslovakia's peaceful transition from communism to capitalist democracy, 1989

**warlord** someone who gets and keeps political power by force

**West** Western Europe and the USA

# Index